Adobe Audition CC
Keyboard Shortcuts

By

U. C-Abel Books.

All Rights Reserved

First Edition: 2017

Table of Contents

Acknowledgement.

All thanks to God Almighty for enabling us to bring this work to this point. He is a wonder indeed.

We want to specially appreciate the great company, Adobe Systems Inc. for their hard work and style of reasoning in providing the public with helpful programs and resources, and for helping us with some of the tips and keyboard shortcuts included in this book.

Dedication

The dedication of this title goes to users of Adobe Audition CC all over the world.

Introduction.

We enjoy using shortcuts because they set us on a high plane that astonishes people around us when we work with them. As wonderful shortcuts users, the worst eyesore we witness in computer operation is to see somebody sluggishly struggling to execute a task through mouse usage when in actual sense shortcuts will help to save that person time. Most people have asked us to help them with a list of keyboard shortcuts that can make them work as smartly as we do and that drove us into research to broaden our knowledge and truly help them as they demanded, that is the reason for the existence of this book. It is a great tool for lovers of shortcuts, and those who want to join the group.

Most times the things we love don't come by easily. It is our love for keyboard shortcuts that made us to bear long sleepless nights like owls just to make sure we get the best out of it, and it is the best we got that we are sharing with you in this book. You cannot be the same at computing after reading this book. The time you entrusted to our care is an expensive possession and we promise not to mess it up.

Thank you.

What to Know Before You Begin.

General Notes.

1. Most of the keyboard shortcuts you will see in this book refer to the U.S. keyboard layout. Keys for other layouts might not correspond exactly to the keys on a U.S. keyboard. Keyboard shortcuts for laptop computers might also differ.

2. It is important to note that when using shortcuts to perform any command, you should make sure the target area is active, if not, you may get a wrong result. Example, if you want to highlight all texts you must make sure the text field is active and if an object, make sure the object area is active. The active area is always known by the location where the cursor of your computer blinks.

3. On a Mac keyboard, the Command key is denoted with the ⌘symbol.

4. If a function key doesn't work on your Mac as you expect it to, press the Fn key in addition to the function key. If you don't want to press the Fn key every time, you can change your Apple system preferences.

5. The plus (+) sign that comes in the middle of keyboard shortcuts simply means the keys are

meant to be combined or held down together not to be added as one of the shortcut keys. In a case where plus sign is needed; it will be duplicated (++).

6. Many keyboards assign special functions to function keys, by default. To use the function key for other purposes, you have to press Fn+the function key.

7. For keyboard shortcuts in which you press one key immediately followed by another key, the keys are separated by a comma (,).

8. For chapters that have more than one topic, search for "A fresh topic" to see the beginning of a topic, and "End of Topic" to see the end of a topic.

9. It is also important to note that the keyboard shortcuts, tips, and techniques listed in this book are for users of Adobe Audition CC.

10. To get more information on this title visit ucabelbooks.wordpress.com and search the site using keywords related to it.

11. Our chief website is under construction.

Some Short Forms You Will Find in This Book and Their Full Meaning.

Here are short forms used in this Adobe Audition CC Keyboard Shortcuts book and their full meaning.

1. Win   -   Windows logo key
2. Tab   -   Tabulate Key
3. Shft   -   Shift Key
4. Prt sc   -   Print Screen
5. Num Lock   -   Number Lock Key
6. F   -   Function Key
7. Esc   -   Escape Key
8. Ctrl   -   Control Key
9. Caps Lock -   Caps Lock Key
10. Alt   -   Alternate Key

CHAPTER 1.

Fundamental Knowledge of Keyboard Shortcuts.

Without the existence of the keyboard, there wouldn't have been anything like keyboard shortcuts so in this chapter we will learn a little about the computer keyboard before moving to keyboard shortcuts.

1. Definition of Computer Keyboard.

This is an input device that is used to send data to computer memory.

Sketch of a Keyboard

1.1 Types of Keyboard.

i. Standard (Basic) Keyboard.
ii. Enhanced (Extended) Keyboard.

i. **Standard Keyboard:** This is a keyboard designed during the 1800s for mechanical typewriters with just 10 function keys (F keys) placed at the left side of it.

ii. **Enhanced Keyboard:** This is the current 101 to 102-key keyboard that is included in almost all the personal computers (PCs) of nowadays, which has 12 function keys, usually at the top side of it.

Function Keys

Numeric Keys

Alphabetic keys

1.2 Segments of the keyboard

- Numeric keys.
- Alphabetic keys.
- Punctuation keys.
- Windows Logo key.
- Function keys.
- Special keys.

Numeric Keys: Numeric keys are keys with numbers from **0 - 9**.

Alphabetic Keys: These are keys that have alphabets on them, ranging from **A** to **Z**.

Punctuation Keys: These are keys of the keyboard used for punctuation, examples include comma, full stop, colon, question marks, hyphen, etc.

Windows Logo Key: A key on Microsoft Computer keyboard with its logo displayed on it. Search for this ⊞ on your keyboard.

Apple Key: This also known as Command key is a modifier key that you can find on an Apple keyboard. It usually has the image of an apple or command logo on it. Search for this on your Apple keyboard ⌘

Function Keys: These are keys that have **F** on them which are usually combined with other keys. They are F1 - F12, and are also in the class called *Special Keys*.

Special Keys: These are keys that perform special functions. They include: Tab, Ctrl, Caps lock, Insert, Prt sc, alt gr, Shift, Home, Num lock, Esc, and many others. Special keys differ according to the type of computer involved. In some keyboard layout, especially laptops, the keys that turn the speaker on/off, the one that increases/decreases volume, the key that turns the computer Wifi on/off are also special keys.

Other Special Keys Worthy of Note.

Enter Key: This is located at the right-hand corner of most keyboards. It is used to send messages to the computer to execute commands, in most cases it is used to mean "Ok" or "Go".

Escape Key (ESC): This is the first key on the upper left of most keyboards. It is used to cancel routines, close menus and select options such as **Save** according to circumstances.

Control Key (CTRL): It is located on the bottom row of the left and right hand side of the keyboard. They also work with the function keys to execute commands using Keyboard shortcuts (key combinations).

Alternate Key (ALT): It is located on the bottom row also of some keyboard, very close to the CTRL key on both side of the keyboard. It enables many editing functions to be accomplished by using some keystroke combinations on the keyboard.

Shift Key: This adds to the roles of function keys. In addition, it enables the use of alternative function of a particular button (key), especially, those with more than one function on a key. E.g. use of capital letters, symbols, and numbers.

1.3. Selecting/Highlighting With Keyboard.

This is a highlighting method or style where data is selected using the computer keyboard instead of a computer mouse.

To do this:

- Move your cursor to the text or object you want to highlight, make sure that area is active,
- Hold down the shift key with one finger,
- Then use another finger to move the arrow key that points to the direction you want to highlight.

1.4 The Operating Modes Of The Keyboard.

Just like the computer mouse, keyboard has two operating modes. The two modes are Text Entering Mode and Command Mode.

a. **Text Entering Mode:** this mode gives the operator/user the opportunity to type text.
b. **Command Mode:** this is used to command the operating system/software/application to execute commands in certain ways.

2. Ways To Improve In Your Typing Skill.

1. Put Your Eyes Off The Keyboard.

This is the aspect of keyboard usage that many don't find funny because they always ask. "How can I put my eyes off the keyboard when I am running away from the occurrence of errors on my file?" My aim is to be fast, is this not going to slow me down?

Of course, there will be errors and at the same time your speed will slow down but the motive behind the introduction to this method is to make you faster than you are. Looking at your keyboard while you type can make you get a sore neck, it is better you learn to touch type because the more you type with your eyes fixed on the screen instead of the keyboard, the faster you become.

An alternative to keeping your eyes off your keyboard is to use the *"Das Keyboard Ultimate"*.

2. Errors Challenge You

It is better to fail than to not try at all. Not trying at all is an attribute of the weak and lazybones. When you make mistakes, try again because errors are opportunities for improvement.

3. Good Posture (Position Yourself Well).

Do not adopt an awkward position while typing. You should get everything on your desk organized or arranged before sitting to type. Your posture while typing contributes to your speed and productivity.

4. Practice

Here is the conclusion of everything said above. You have to practice your shortcuts constantly. The practice alone is a way of improvement. "Practice brings improvement". Practice always.

2.1 Software That Will Help You Improve Your Typing Skill.

There are several Software programs for typing that both kids and adults can use for their typing skill. Here is a list of software that can help you improve in your typing: Mavis Beacon, Typing Instructor, Mucky Typing Adventure, Rapid Tying Tutor, Letter Chase Tying Tutor, Alice Touch Typing Tutor and many more. Personally, I love Mavis Beacon.

To learn typing using MAVIS BEACON, install Mavis Beacon software to your computer, start with keyboard lesson, then move to games. Games like **_Penguin Crossing, Creature Lab_**, or **_Space Junk_** will help you become a professional in typing. Typing and keyboard shortcuts work hand-in-hand.

Sketch of a computer mouse

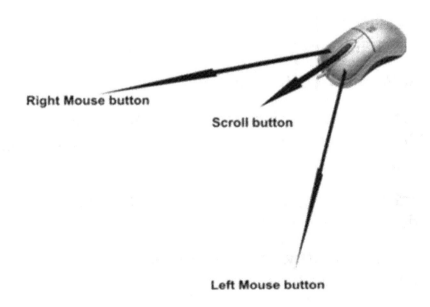

Right Mouse button

Scroll button

Left Mouse button

3. Mouse:

This is an oval-shaped portable input device with three buttons for scrolling, left clicking, and right clicking that enables work to be done effectively on a computer. The plural form of mouse is mice.

3.1 Types of Computer Mouse

- Mechanical Mouse.
- Optical Mechanical Mouse (Optomechanical).
- Laser Mouse.

- Optical Mouse.
- BlueTrack Mouse.

3.2 Forms of Clicking:

Left Clicking: This is the process of clicking the left side button of the mouse. It can also be called *clicking* without the addition of *left*.

Right Clicking: It is the process of clicking the right side button of a computer mouse.

Double Clicking: It is the process of clicking the left side button two times (twice) and immediately.

Triple Clicking: It is the process of clicking the left side button three times (thrice) and immediately.

Double clicking is used to select a word while triple clicking is used to select a sentence or paragraph.

Scroll Button: It is the little key attached to the mouse that looks like a tiny wheel. It takes you up and down a page when moved.

3.3 Mouse Pad: This is a small soft mat that is placed under the mouse to make it have a free movement.

3.4 Laptop Mouse Touchpad

This unlike the mouse we explained above is not external, rather it is inbuilt (comes with the laptop computer). With the presence of a laptop mouse touchpad, an external mouse is not needed to use a laptop, except in a case where it is malfunctioning or the operator prefers to use external one for some reasons.

The laptop mouse touchpad is usually positioned at the end of the keyboard section of a laptop computer. It is rectangular in shape with two buttons positioned below it. The two buttons/keys are used for left and right clicking just like the external mouse. Some laptops come with four mouse keys. Two placed above the mouse for left and right clicking and two other keys placed below it for the same function.

4. Definition Of Keyboard Shortcuts.

Keyboard shortcuts are defined as a series of keys, most times with combination that execute tasks which typically involve the use of mouse or other input devices.

5. Why You Should Use Shortcuts.

1. One may not be able to use a computer mouse easily because of disability or pain.

2. One may not be able to see the mouse pointer as a result of vision impairment, in such case what will the person do? The answer is SHORTCUT.

3. Research has made it known that Extensive mouse usage is related to Repetitive Syndrome Injury (RSI) greatly than the use of keyboard.

4. Keyboard shortcuts speed up computer users, making learning them a worthwhile effort.

5. When performing a job that requires precision, it is wise that you use the keyboard instead of mouse, for instance, if you are dealing with Text Editing, it is better you handle it using keyboard shortcuts than spending more time doing it with your computer mouse alone.

6. Studies calculate that using keyboard shortcuts allows working 10 times faster than working with the mouse. The time you spend looking for the mouse and then getting the cursor to the position you want is lost! Reducing your work duration by 10 times gives you greater results.

5.1 Ways To Become A Lover Of Shortcuts.

1. Always have the urge to learn new shortcut keys associated with the programs you use.
2. Be happy whenever you learn a new shortcut.

3. Try as much as you can to apply the new shortcuts you learnt.
4. Always bear it in mind that learning new shortcuts is worth it.
5. Always remember that the use of keyboard shortcuts keeps people healthy while performing computer activities.

5.2 How To Learn New Shortcut Keys
1. Do a research on them: quick references (a cheat sheet comprehensively compiled like ours) can go a long way to help you improve.
2. Buy applications that show you keyboard shortcuts every time you execute an action with mouse.
3. Disconnect your mouse if you must learn this fast.
4. Read user manuals and help topics (Whether offline or online).

5.3 Your Reward For Knowing Shortcut Keys.
1. You will get faster unimaginably.
2. Your level of efficiency will increase.
3. You will find it easy to use.
4. Opportunities are high that you will become an expert in what you do.
5. You won't have to go for **Office button**, click **New,** click **Blank and Recent**, and click **Create**

just to insert a fresh/blank page. **Ctrl +N** takes care of that in a second.

A Funny Note: Keyboarding and Mousing are in a marital union with Keyboarding being the head, so it will be unfair for anybody to put asunder between them.

5.4 Why We Emphasize On The Use of Shortcuts.

You may never leave your mouse completely unless you are ready to make your brain a box of keyboard shortcuts which will really be frustrating, just imagine yourself learning all shortcuts that go with the programs you use and their various versions. You shouldn't learn keyboard shortcuts that way.

Why we are emphasizing on the use of shortcuts is because mouse usage is becoming unusually common and unhealthy, too. So we just want to make sure both are combined so you can get fast, productive and healthy in your computer activities. All you need to know is just the most important ones associated with the programs you use.

CHAPTER 2.

15 (Fifteen) Special Keyboard Shortcuts.

The fifteen special keyboard shortcuts are fifteen (15) shortcuts every computer user should know.

The following is a list of keyboard shortcuts every computer user should know:

1. **Ctrl + A:** Control A, highlights or selects everything you have in the environment where you are working.

   *If you are like **"Wow, the content of this document is large and there is no time to select all of it, besides, it's going to mount pressure on my computer?"** Using the mouse for this is an outdated method of handling a task like selecting all, Ctrl+A will take care of that in a second.*

2. **Ctrl + C:** Control C copies any highlighted or selected element within the work environment.
   Saves the time and stress which would have been used to right click and click again just to copy. Use ctrl+c.

3. **Ctrl + N:** Control N opens a new window or file.
   Instead of clicking **File, New, blank/ template** *and another* **click,** *just press* **Ctrl + N** *and a fresh page or window will appear instantly.*

4. **Ctrl + O:** Control O opens a new program.
   Use ctrl +O when you want to locate / open a file or program.

5. **Ctrl + P:** Control P prints the active document.
   Always use this to locate the printer dialog box, and thereafter print.

6. **Ctrl + S:** Control S saves a new document or file and changes made by the user.
   Please stop! Don't use the mouse. Just press Ctrl+S and everything will be saved.

7. **Ctrl +V:** Control V pastes copied elements into the active area of the program in use.

Using ctrl+V in a case like this Saves the time and stress of right clicking and clicking again just to paste.

8. **Ctrl + W:** Control W is used to close the page you are working on when you want to leave the work environment.

   "There is a way Debby does this without using the mouse. Oh my God, why didn't I learn it then?" Don't worry, I have the answer. Debby presses Ctrl+W to close active windows.

9. **Ctrl + X:** Control X cuts elements (making the elements to disappear from their original place). The difference between cutting and deleting elements is that in Cutting, what was cut doesn't get lost permanently but prepares itself so that it can be pasted on another location defined by the user.

   Use ctrl+x when you think ***"this shouldn't be here and I can't stand the stress of retyping or redesigning it on the rightful place it belongs".***

10. **Ctrl + Y:** Control Y undoes already done actions.

    Ctrl+Z brought back what you didn't need? Press Ctrl+ Y to remove it again.

17

11. **Ctrl + Z:** Control Z redoes actions.
    Can't find what you typed now or a picture you inserted, it suddenly disappeared or you mistakenly removed it? Press Ctrl+Z to bring it back.

12. **Alt + F4:** Alternative F4 closes active windows or items.

    *You don't need to move the mouse in order to close an active window, just press **Alt + F4**. Also use it when you are done or you don't want somebody who is coming to see what you are doing.*

13. **Ctrl + F6:** Control F6 Navigates between open windows, making it possible for a user to see what is happening in windows that are active.
    Are you working in Microsoft Word and want to find out if the other active window where your browser is loading a page is still progressing? Use Ctrl + F6.

14. **F1:** This displays the help window.

    *Is your computer malfunctioning? Use **F1** to find help when you don't know what next to do.*

15. **F12:** This enables user to make changes to an already saved document.

   F12 is the shortcut to use when you want to change the format in which you saved your existing document, password it, change its name, change the file location or destination, or make other changes to it. It will save you time.

Note: The Control (Ctrl) key on Windows and Linux operating system is the same thing as Command (Cmmd) key on a Macintosh computer. So if you replace Control with Command key on a Mac computer for the special shortcuts listed above, you will get the same result.

CHAPTER 3.

Tips, Tricks, Techniques, and Keyboard Shortcuts for use in Adobe Audition CC.

About the application: This, formerly known as Cool Edit Pro, is an application used for recording and mixing audio for video, podcasting, and sound effect design; developed, maintained and marketed by Adobe Systems Incorporated.

A fresh topic ⌐→

Noise Reduction Techniques and Restoration Effects for Audition.

Techniques for Restoring Audio.

You can fix a wide array of audio problems by combining two powerful features. First, use Spectral Display to visually identify and select ranges of noise or individual artifacts. Then, use either Diagnostic or

Noise Reduction effects to fix problems like the following:

- Crackle from wireless microphones or old vinyl records. (See Automatic Click Remover effect.)
- Background noise like wind rumble, tape hiss, or power-line hum. (See Adaptive Noise Reduction effect and DeHummer effect.)
- Phase cancelation from poorly placed stereo microphones or misaligned tape machines. (See Automatic Phase Correction effect.)

Note:

The real-time restoration effects above, which are available in both the Waveform and Multitrack editors, quickly address common audio problems. For unusually noisy audio, however, consider using offline, process effects unique to the Waveform Editor, such as Hiss Reduction and Noise Reduction.

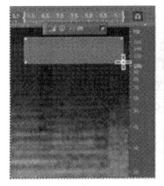  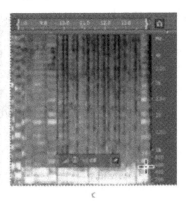

Selecting various types of noise in Spectral Display

A. Hiss B. Crackle C. Rumble

Noise Reduction Effect (Waveform Editor only).

The Noise Reduction/Restoration > Noise Reduction effect dramatically reduces background and broadband noise with a minimal reduction in signal quality. This effect can remove a combination of noise, including tape hiss, microphone background noise, power-line hum, or any noise that is constant throughout a waveform.

The proper amount of noise reduction depends upon the type of background noise and the acceptable loss in quality for the remaining signal. In general, you can increase the signal-to-noise ratio by 5 to 20 dB and retain high audio quality.

To achieve the best results with the Noise Reduction effect, apply it to audio with no DC offset. With a DC offset, this effect may introduce clicks in quiet passages. (To remove a DC offset, choose Favorites > Repair DC Offset.)

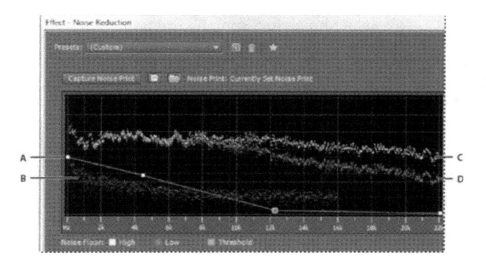

Evaluating and adjusting noise with the Noise Reduction graph:

A. Drag control points to vary reduction in different frequency ranges **B.** Low amplitude noise. **C.** High amplitude noise **D.** Threshold below which noise reduction occurs.

Apply the Noise Reduction effect

1. In the Waveform Editor, select a range that contains only noise and is at least half a second long.

   Note:

To select noise in a specific frequency range, use the Marquee Selection tool.

2. Choose Effects > Noise Reduction/Restoration > Capture Noise Print.
3. In the Editor panel, select the range from which you want to remove noise.
4. Choose Effects > Noise Reduction/Restoration > Noise Reduction.
5. Set the desired options.

Note:

When recording in noisy environments, record a few seconds of representative background noise that can be used as a noise print later on.

NOISE Reduction options

Capture Noise Print

Extracts a noise profile from a selected range, indicating only background noise. Adobe Audition gathers statistical information about the background noise so it can remove it from the remainder of the waveform.

Tip: If the selected range is too short, Capture Noise Print is disabled. Reduce the FFT Size or select a longer range of noise. If you can't find a longer range, copy and paste the currently selected range to create one. (You can later remove the pasted noise by using the Edit > Delete command.)

Save the Current Noise Print

Saves the noise print as an .fft file, which contains information about sample type, FFT (Fast Fourier Transform) size, and three sets of FFT coefficients: one for the lowest amount of noise found, one for the highest amount, and one for the power average.

Load a Noise Print from Disk

Opens any noise print previously saved from Adobe Audition in FFT format. However, you can apply noise prints only to identical sample types. (For example, you can't apply a 22 kHz mono profile to 44kHz stereo samples.)

Note: *Because noise prints are so specific, a print for one type of noise won't produce good results with other types. If you regularly remove similar noise, however, a saved profile can greatly increase efficiency.*

Graph

Depicts frequency along the x-axis (horizontal) and the amount of noise reduction along the y-axis (vertical).

The blue control curve sets the amount of noise reduction in different frequency ranges. For example, if you need noise reduction only in the higher frequencies, adjust the control curve downward to the right of the graph.

If you click the Reset button 🔄 to flatten the control curve, the amount of noise reduction is based entirely on the noise print.

Tip: To better focus on the noise floor, click the menu button ⊟ to the upper right of the graph, and deselect Show Control Curve and Show Tooltip Over Graph.

Noise Floor

High shows the highest amplitude of detected noise at each frequency; Low shows the lowest amplitude. Threshold shows the amplitude below which noise reduction occurs.

Tip: The three elements of the noise floor can overlap in the graph. To better distinguish them, click the menu button ⊟, and select options from the Show Noise Floor menu.

Scale

Determines how frequencies are arranged along the horizontal x-axis:

- For finer control over low frequencies, select Logarithmic. A logarithmic scale more closely resembles how people hear sound.
- For detailed, high-frequency work with evenly spaced intervals in frequency, select Linear.

Channel

Displays the selected channel in the graph. The amount of noise reduction is always the same for all channels.

Select Entire File

Lets you apply a captured noise print to the entire file.

Noise Reduction

Controls the percentage of noise reduction in the output signal. Fine-tune this setting while previewing audio to achieve maximum noise reduction with minimum artifacts. (Excessively high noise reduction levels can sometimes cause audio to sound flanged or out-of-phase.)

Reduce By

Determines the amplitude reduction of detected noise. Values between 6 and 30 dB work well. To reduce bubbly artifacts, enter lower values.

Output Noise Only

Previews only noise so you determine if the effect is removing any desirable audio.

Advanced settings

Click the triangle to display the following options:

Spectral Decay Rate

Specifies the percentage of frequencies processed when audio falls below the noise floor. Fine-tuning this percentage allows greater noise reduction with fewer artifacts. Values of 40% to 75% work best. Below those values, bubbly-sounding artifacts are often heard; above those values, excessive noise typically remains.

Smoothing

Takes into account the variance of the noise signal in each frequency band. Bands that vary greatly when analyzed (such as white noise) will be smoothed differently than constant bands (like 60-Hz hum). In general, increasing the smoothing amount (up to 2 or so) reduces burbly background artifacts at the expense of raising the overall background broadband noise level.

Precision Factor

Controls changes in amplitude. Values of 5-10 work best, and odd numbers are ideal for symmetrical processing. With values of 3 or less, the Fast Fourier transform is performed in giant blocks, and between them drops or spikes in volume can occur. Values beyond 10 cause no noticeable change in quality, but they increase processing time.

Transition Width

Determines the amplitude range between noise and desirable audio. For example, a width of zero applies a sharp, noise gate to each frequency band. Audio just above the threshold remains; audio just below is truncated to silence. Alternatively, you can specify a range over which the audio fades to silence based upon the input level. For example, if the transition width is 10 dB, and the noise level for the band is -60 dB, audio at -60 dB stays the same, audio at -62 dB is reduced slightly, and audio at -70 dB is removed entirely.

FFT Size

Determines how many individual frequency bands are analyzed. This option causes the most drastic changes in quality. The noise in each frequency band is treated separately, so with more bands, noise is removed with finer frequency detail. Good settings range from 4096 to 8192.

Fast Fourier Transform size determines the tradeoff between frequency- and time-accuracy. Higher FFT sizes might cause swooshing or reverberant artifacts, but they very accurately remove noise frequencies. Lower FFT sizes result in better time response (less swooshing before cymbal hits, for example), but they can produce poorer frequency resolution, creating hollow or flanged sounds.

Noise Print Snapshots

Determines how many snapshots of noise to include in the captured profile. A value of 4000 is optimal for producing accurate data.

Very small values greatly affect the quality of the various noise reduction levels. With more snapshots, a noise reduction level of 100 will likely cut out more noise, but also cut out more original signal. However, a low noise reduction level with more snapshots will also cut out more noise, but likely retain the intended signal.

Sound Remover Effect.

The Sound Remover effect (**Effects > Noise Reduction/Restoration**) removes unwanted audio sources from a recording. This effect analyzes a selected portion of the recording, and builds a sound model, which is used to find and remove the sound.

The generated model can also be modified using parameters that indicate its complexity. A high complexity sound model requires more refinement passes to process the recording, but provides more accurate results. You can also save the sound model for later use. Several common presets are also included to remove some common noise sounds, such as sirens and ringing mobile phones.

Learn Sound Model

Uses the selected waveform to learn the sound model. Select an area on the waveform that only contains the sound to remove, and then press Learn Sound Model. You can also save and load sound models on disc.

Sound Model Complexity

Indicates the complexity of the Sound Model. The more complex or mixed the sound is, the better results you'll get with a higher complexity setting, though the longer it will take to calculate. Settings range from 1 to 100.

Sound Refinement Passes

Defines the number of refinement passes to make to remove the sound patterns indicated in the sound model. Higher number of passes require longer processing time, but offer more accurate results.

Content Complexity

Indicates the complexity of the signal. The more complex or mixed the sound is, the better results you'll get with a higher complexity setting, though the longer it will take to calculate. Settings range from 5 to 100.

Content Refinement Passes

Specifies the number of passes to make on the content to remove the sounds that match the sound model. A higher number of passes require more processing time, but generally provide more accurate results.

Enhanced Supression

This increases the aggressiveness of the sound removal algorithm, and can be modified on the Strength value. A higher value will remove more of the sound model from mixed signals, which can result in greater loss of desired signal, while a lower value will leave more of the overlapping signal and therefore, more of the noise may be audible (though less than the original recording.)

Enhance for Speech

Specifies that the audio includes speech and is careful in removing audio patterns that closely resemble speech. The end result makes sure that speech is not removed, while removing noise.

FFT Size

Determines how many individual frequency bands are analyzed. This option causes the most drastic changes in quality. The noise in each frequency band is treated separately, so with more bands, noise is removed with finer frequency detail. Good settings range from 4096 to   8192. Fast Fourier Transform size determines the tradeoff between frequency- and time-accuracy. Higher FFT sizes might cause swooshing or reverberant artifacts, but they very accurately remove noise frequencies. Lower FFT sizes result in better time response (less swooshing before cymbal hits, for example), but they can produce poorer frequency resolution, creating hollow or flanged sounds.

Adaptive Noise Reduction Effect.

The Noise Reduction/Restoration > Adaptive Noise Reduction effect quickly removes variable broadband noise such as background sounds, rumble, and wind. Because this effect operates in real time, you can combine it with other effects in the Effects Rack and apply it in the Multitrack Editor. By contrast, the standard Noise Reduction effect is available only as an offline process in the Waveform Editor. That effect, however, is sometimes more effective at removing constant noise, such as hiss or hum.

For best results, apply Adaptive Noise Reduction to selections that begin with noise followed by desirable audio. The effect identifies noise based on the first few seconds of audio.

Note:

This effect requires significant processing. If your system performs slowly, lower FFT Size and turn off High Quality Mode.

Reduce Noise By

Determines the level of noise reduction. Values between 6 and 30 dB work well. To reduce bubbly background effects, enter lower values.

Noisiness

Indicates the percentage of original audio that contains noise.

Fine Tune Noise Floor

Manually adjusts the noise floor above or below the automatically calculated floor.

Signal Threshold

Manually adjusts the threshold of desirable audio above or below the automatically calculated threshold.

Spectral Decay Rate

Determines how quickly noise processing drops by 60 decibels. Fine-tuning this setting allows greater noise reduction with fewer artifacts. Values that are too short create bubbly sounds; values that are too long create a reverb effect.

Broadband Preservation

Retains desirable audio in specified frequency bands between found artifacts. A setting of 100 Hz, for example, ensures that no audio is removed 100 Hz above or below found artifacts. Lower settings remove more noise but may introduce audible processing.

FFT Size

Determines how many individual frequency bands are analyzed. Choose a high setting to increase frequency resolution; choose a low setting to increase time resolution. High settings work well for artifacts of long duration (like squeaks or power-line hum), while low settings better address transient artifacts (like clicks and pops).

Automatic Click Remover Effect.

To quickly remove crackle and static from vinyl recordings, use the Noise Reduction/Restoration > Automatic Click Remover effect. You can correct a large area of audio or a single click or pop.

This effect provides the same options as the DeClicker effect, which lets you choose which detected clicks to address (see DeClicker options). However, because the Automatic Click Remover operates in real time, you can combine it with other effects in the Effects Rack and apply it in the Multitrack Editor. The Automatic Click Remover effect also applies multiple scan and repair passes automatically; to achieve the same level of click reduction with the DeClicker, you must manually apply it multiple times.

Threshold

Determines sensitivity to noise. Lower settings detect more clicks and pops but may include audio you wish to retain. Settings range from 1 to 100; the default is 30.

Complexity

Indicates the complexity of noise. Higher settings apply more processing but can degrade audio quality. Settings range from 1 to 100; the default is 16.

Automatic Phase Correction Effect.

The Noise Reduction/Restoration > Automatic Phase Correction effect addresses azimuth errors from misaligned tape heads, stereo smearing from incorrect microphone placement, and many other phase-related problems.

Global Time Shift

Activates the Left and Right Channel Shift sliders, which let you apply a uniform phase shift to all selected audio.

Auto Align Channels and Auto Center Panning

Align phase and panning for a series of discrete time intervals, which you specify using the following options:

Time Resolution

Specifies the number of milliseconds in each processed interval. Smaller values increase accuracy; larger ones increase performance.

Responsiveness

Determines overall processing speed. Slow settings increase accuracy; fast settings increase performance.

Channel

Specifies the channels phase correction will be applied to.

Analysis Size

Specifies the number of samples in each analyzed unit of audio.

Note:

For the most precise, effective phase correction, use the Auto Align Channels option. Enable the Global Time Shift sliders only if you are confident that a uniform adjustment is necessary, or if you want to manually animate phase correction in the Multitrack Editor.

Click/Pop Eliminator Effect.

Use the **Click/Pop Eliminator** effect (**Effects > Noise Reduction/Restoration**) to remove microphone pops, clicks, light hiss, and crackles. Such noise is common on recordings such as old vinyl records and on-location recordings. The effect dialog box stays open, and you can adjust the selection, and fix multiple clicks without reopening the effect several times.

Detection and correction settings are used to find clicks and pops. The detection and rejection ranges are displayed graphically.

Detection graph

Shows the exact threshold levels to be used at each amplitude, with amplitude along the horizontal ruler (x-axis) and threshold level along the vertical ruler (y-axis). Adobe Audition uses values on the curve to the right (above -20 dB or so) when processing louder audio and values on the left when processing softer audio. Curves are color-coded to indicate detection and rejection.

Scan for All Levels

Scans the highlighted area for clicks based on the values for Sensitivity and Discrimination, and determines values for Threshold, Detect, and Reject. Five areas of audio are selected, starting at the quietest and moving to the loudest.

Sensitivity

Determines the level of clicks to detect. Use a lower value, such as 10, to detect lots of subtle clicks, or a value of 20 to detect a few louder clicks. (Detected levels with Scan for All Levels are always higher than with this option.)

Discrimination

Determines how many clicks to fix. Enter high values to fix very few clicks and leave most of the original audio intact. Enter lower values, such as 20 or 40, if the audio contains a moderate number of clicks. Enter extremely low values, such as 2 or 4, to fix constant clicks.

Scan for Threshold Levels

Automatically sets the Maximum, Average, and Minimum Threshold levels.

Maximum, Average, Minimum

Determine the unique detection and rejection thresholds for the maximum, average, and minimum amplitudes of the audio. For example, if audio has a maximum RMS amplitude of -10 dB, you should set Maximum Threshold to -10 dB. If the minimum RMS amplitude is -55 dB, then set Minimum Threshold to -55.

Set the threshold levels before you adjust the corresponding Detect and Reject values. (Set the Maximum and Minimum Threshold levels first, because once they're in place, you shouldn't need to adjust them much.) Set the Average Threshold level to about three quarters of the way between the Maximum and Minimum Threshold levels. For example, if Maximum Threshold is set to 30 and Minimum Threshold is set to 10, set Average Threshold to 25.

After you audition a small piece of repaired audio, you can adjust the settings as needed. For example, if a quiet part still has a lot of clicks, lower the Minimum Threshold level a bit. If a loud piece still has clicks, lower the Average or Maximum Threshold level. In general, less correction is required for louder audio, as the audio itself masks many clicks, so repairing them isn't necessary. Clicks are very noticeable in very quiet audio, so quiet audio tends to require lower detection and rejection thresholds.

Second Level Verification (Reject Clicks)

Rejects some of the potential clicks found by the click detection algorithm. In some types of audio, such as trumpets, saxophones, female vocals, and snare drum hits, normal peaks are sometimes detected as clicks. If these peaks are corrected, the resulting audio will sound muffled. Second Level Verification rejects these audio peaks and corrects only true clicks.

Detect

Determines sensitivity to clicks and pops. Possible values range from 1 to 150, but recommended values range from 6 to 60. Lower values detect more clicks.

Start with a threshold of 35 for high-amplitude audio (above -15 dB), 25 for average amplitudes, and 10 for low-amplitude audio (below-50 dB). These settings allow for the most clicks to be found, and usually all of the louder ones. If a constant crackle is in the background of the source audio, try lowering the Min Threshold level or increasing the dB level to which the threshold is assigned. The level can be as low as 6, but a lower setting can cause the filter to remove sound other than clicks.

If more clicks are detected, more repair occurs, increasing the possibility of distortion. With too much distortion of this type, audio begins to sound flat and lifeless. If this occurs, set the detection threshold rather low, and select Second Level Verification to reanalyze the detected clicks and disregard percussive transients that aren't clicks.

Reject

Determines how many potential clicks (found using the Detection Threshold) are rejected if Second Level Verification box is selected. Values range from 1 to 100; a setting of 30 is a good starting point. Lower settings allow for more clicks to be repaired. Higher settings can prevent clicks from being repaired, as they might not be actual clicks.

You want to reject as many detected clicks as possible but still remove all audible clicks. If a trumpet-like sound has clicks in it, and the clicks aren't removed, try lowering the value to reject fewer potential clicks. If a particular sound becomes distorted, then increase the setting to keep repairs at a minimum. (The fewer repairs that are needed to get good results, the better.)

FFT Size

Determines the FFT size used to repair clicks, pops, and crackle. In general, select Auto to let Adobe Audition determine the FFT size. For some types of audio, however, you might want to enter a specific FFT size (from 8 to 512). A good starting value is 32, but if clicks are still quite audible, increase the value to 48, and then 64, and so on. The higher the value, the slower the correction will be, but the better the potential results. If the value is too high, rumbly, low frequency distortion can occur.

Fill Single Click

Corrects a single click in a selected audio range. If Auto is selected next to FFT Size, then an appropriate FFT size is used for the restoration based on the size of the area being restored. Otherwise, settings of 128 to 256 work very well for filling in single clicks. Once a single click is filled, press the F3 key to repeat the action. You can also create a quick key in the Favorites menu for filling in single clicks.

Pop Oversamples Width

Includes surrounding samples in detected clicks. When a potential click is found, its beginning and end points are marked as closely as possible. The Pop Oversamples value (which can range from 0 to 300) expands that range, so more samples to the left and right of the click are considered part of the click. If corrected clicks become quieter but are still evident, increase the Pop oversamples value. Start with a value of 8, and increase it slowly to as much as 30 or 40. Audio that doesn't contain a click shouldn't change very much if it's corrected, so this buffer area should remain mostly untouched by the replacement algorithm.
Increasing the Pop Oversamples value also forces larger FFT sizes to be used if Auto is selected. A larger setting may remove clicks more cleanly, but if it's too high, audio will start to distort where the clicks are removed.

Run Size

Specifies the number of samples between separate clicks. Possible values range from 0 to 1000. To independently correct extremely close clicks, enter a low value; clicks that occur within the Run Size range are corrected together.

A good starting point is around 25 (or half the FFT size if Auto next to FFT Size isn't selected). If the Run Size value is too large (over 100 or so), then the corrections may become more noticeable, as very large blocks of data are repaired at once. If you set the Run Size too small, then clicks that are very close together may not be repaired completely on the first pass.

Pulse Train Verification

Prevents normal waveform peaks from being detected as clicks. It may also reduce detection of valid clicks, requiring more aggressive threshold settings. Select this option only if you've already tried to clean up the audio but stubborn clicks remain.

Link Channels

Processes all channels equally, preserving the stereo or surround balance. For example, if a click is found in one channel, a click will most likely be detected in the other.

Detect Big Pops

Removes large unwanted events (such as those more than a few hundred samples wide) that might not be detected as clicks. Values can range from 30 to 200.

Note that a sharp sound like a loud snare drum hit can have the same characteristic as a very large pop, so select this option only if you know the audio has very large pops (like a vinyl record with a very big scratch in it). If this option causes drum hits to sound softer, slightly increase the threshold to fix only loud, obvious pops.

If loud, obvious pops aren't fixed, select Detect Big Pops, and use settings from about 30 (to find quiet pops) to 70 (to find loud pops).

Ignore Light Crackle

Smooths out one-sample errors when detected, often removing more background crackle. If the resulting audio sounds thinner, flatter, or tinnier, deselect this option.

Passes

Performs up to 32 passes automatically to catch clicks that might be too close together to be repaired effectively. Fewer passes occur if no more clicks are found and all detected clicks are repaired. In general, about half as many clicks are repaired on each successive pass. A higher detection threshold might lead to fewer repairs and increase the quality while still removing all clicks.

DeHummer effect

The Noise Reduction/Restoration > DeHummer effect removes narrow frequency bands and their harmonics. The most common application addresses power line hum from lighting and electronics. But the DeHummer can also apply a notch filter that removes an overly resonant frequency from source audio.

Note:

To quickly address typical audio problems, choose an option from the Presets menu.

Frequency

Sets the root frequency of the hum. If you're unsure of the precise frequency, drag this setting back and forth while previewing audio.

Note:

To visually adjust root frequency and gain, drag directly in the graph.

Q

Sets the width of the root frequency and harmonics above. Higher values affect a narrower range of frequencies, and lower values affect a wider range.

Gain

Determines the amount of hum attenuation.

Number of Harmonics

Specifies how many harmonic frequencies to affect.

Harmonic Slope

Changes the attenuation ratio for harmonic frequencies.

Output Hum Only

Lets you preview removed hum to determine if it contains any desirable audio.

Hiss Reduction effect (Waveform Editor only).

The Noise Reduction/Restoration > Hiss Reduction effect reduces hiss from sources such as audio cassettes, vinyl records, or microphone preamps. This effect greatly lowers the amplitude of a frequency range if it falls below an amplitude threshold called the *noise floor*. Audio in frequency ranges that are louder than the threshold remain untouched. If audio has a consistent level of background hiss, that hiss can be removed completely.

Note:

To reduce other types of noise that have a wide frequency range, try the Noise Reduction effect.

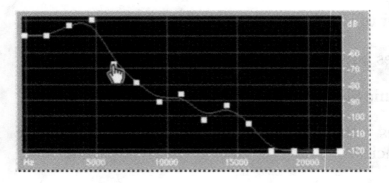

Using the Hiss Reduction graph to adjust the noise floor.

Capture Noise Floor

Graphs an estimate of the noise floor. The estimate is used by the Hiss Reduction effect to more effectively remove only hiss while leaving regular audio untouched. This option is the most powerful feature of Hiss Reduction.

To create a graph that most accurately reflects the noise floor, click Get Noise Floor with a selection of audio that contains only hiss. Or, select an area that has the least amount of desirable audio, in addition to the least amount of high frequency information. (In the spectral display, look for an area without any activity in the top 75% of the display.)

After you capture the noise floor, you might need to lower the control points on the left (representing the lower frequencies) to make the graph as flat as possible. If music is present at any frequency, the control points around that frequency will be higher than they should be.

Graph

Represents the estimated noise floor for each frequency in the source audio, with frequency along the horizontal ruler (x-axis) and the amplitude of the noise floor along the vertical ruler (y-axis). This information helps you distinguish hiss from desirable audio data.

The actual value used to perform hiss reduction is a combination of the graph and the Noise Floor slider, which shifts the estimated noise floor reading up or down for fine-tuning.

Note:

To disable tooltips for frequency and amplitude, click the menu button ▣ to the upper right of the graph, and deselect Show Tooltip Over Graph.

Scale

Determines how frequencies are arranged along the horizontal x-axis:

- For finer control over low frequencies, select Logarithmic. A logarithmic scale more closely resembles how people hear sound.
- For detailed, high-frequency work with evenly spaced intervals in frequency, select Linear.

Channel

Displays the selected audio channel in the graph.

Reset

Resets the estimated noise floor. To reset the floor higher or lower, click the menu button ▤ to the upper right of the graph, and choose an option from the Reset Control Curve menu.

Note:

For quick, general-purpose hiss reduction, a complete noise floor graph isn't always necessary. In many cases, you can simply reset the graph to an even level and manipulate the Noise Floor slider.

Noise Floor

Fine-tunes the noise floor until the appropriate level of hiss reduction and quality is achieved.

Reduce By

Sets the level of hiss reduction for audio below the noise floor. With higher values (especially above 20 dB) dramatic hiss reduction can be achieved, but the remaining audio might become distorted. With lower values, not as much noise is removed, and the original audio signal stays relatively undisturbed.

Output Hiss Only

Lets you preview only hiss to determine if the effect is removing any desirable audio.

Advanced settings

Click the triangle to display these options:

Spectral Decay Rate

When audio is encountered above the estimated noise floor, determines how much audio in surrounding frequencies is assumed to follow. With low values, less audio is assumed to follow, and hiss reduction will cut more closely to the frequencies being kept.

Values of 40% to 75% work best. If the value is too high (above 90%), unnaturally long tails and reverbs might be heard. If the value is too low, background bubbly effects might be heard, and music might sound artificial.

Precision Factor

Determines the time-accuracy of hiss reduction. Typical values range from 7 to 14. Lower values might result in a few milliseconds of hiss before and after louder parts of audio. Larger values generally produce better results and slower processing speeds. Values over 20 don't ordinarily improve quality any further.

Transition Width

Produces a slow transition in hiss reduction instead of an abrupt change. Values from 5 to 10 usually achieve good results. If the value is too high, some hiss may remain after processing. If the value is too low, background artifacts might be heard.

FFT Size

Specifies a Fast Fourier Transform size, which determines the tradeoff between frequency- and time-accuracy. In general, sizes from 2048 to 8192 work best.

Lower FFT sizes (2048 and below) result in better time response (less swooshing before cymbal hits, for example), but they can produce poorer frequency resolution, creating hollow or flanged sounds.

Higher FFT sizes (8192 and above) might cause swooshing, reverb, and drawn out background tones, but they produce very accurate frequency resolution.

Control Points

Specifies the number of points added to the graph when you click Capture Noise Floor.

End of Topic.

A fresh topic

Default Keyboard Shortcuts in Audition CC .

Use the following list of keyboard shortcuts to enhance your productivity in Adobe Audition.

Keys for Playing and Zooming Audio.

Result	Windows Shortcut	Mac OS Shortcut
Toggle between	8	8

Waveform and Multitrack Editor		
Start and stop playback	Spacebar	Spacebar
Move current-time indicator to beginning of timeline	Home	Home
Move current-time indicator to end of timeline	End	End
Move current-time indicator to previous marker, clip, or selection edge	Ctrl+left arrow	Command+left arrow
Move current-	Ctrl+right arrow	Command+right arrow

time indicator to next marker, clip, or selection edge		
Toggle preference for Return CTI To Start Position On Stop	Shift+X	Shift+X
Zoom in horizontally	=	=
Zoom in vertically	Alt+=	Option+=
Zoom out horizontally	-	-
Zoom out vertically	Alt+minus sign	Option+minus sign
Add marker	M or * (asterisk)	M or * (asterisk)
Move to previous marker	Crtl+Alt+left arrow	Cmd+Option+left arrow

Move to next marker	Crtl+Alt+right arrow	Cmd+Option+right arrow

Keys for Editing Audio Files.

The following keyboard shortcuts apply only in the Waveform Editor.

Result	Windows Shortcut	Mac OS Shortcut
Repeat previous command (opening its dialog box and clicking OK)	Shift+R	Shift+R
Repeat previous command (opening its dialog box but not clicking OK)	Ctrl+R	Command+R
Open Convert Sample	Shift+T	Shift+T

Type dialog box		
Capture a noise reduction profile for the Noise Reduction effect	Shift+P	Shift+P
Activate left channel of a stereo file for editing	Up arrow	Up arrow
Activate right channel of a stereo file for editing	Down arrow	Down arrow
Make spectral display more logarithmic or linear	Ctrl+Alt+up or down arrow	Option+Command+up or down arrow
Make spectral display fully logarithmic or linear	Ctrl+Alt+Page Up or Down	Option+Command+Page Up or Down

Increase or decrease spectral resolution	Shift+Ctrl+up or down arrow	Shift+Command-up or down arrow

Keys for Mixing Multitrack Sessions.

The following keyboard shortcuts apply only in the Multitrack Editor.

Result	Windows Shortcut	Mac OS Shortcut
Select the same input or output for all audio tracks	Ctrl+Shift-select	Command+Shift-select
Activate or deactivate Mute, Solo, Arm For Record, or Monitor Input in all tracks	Ctrl+Shift-click	Command+Shift-click
Adjust knobs in large increments	Shift-drag	Shift-drag
Adjust knobs in small increments	Ctrl-drag	Command-drag
Nudge selected clip to the left	Alt+comma	Option+comma
Nudge selected clip to the right	Alt+period	Alt+period

Maintain keyframe time position or parameter value	Shift-drag	Shift-drag
Reposition envelope segment without creating keyframe	Ctrl-drag	Command-drag

Applies to: *Adobe Audition CC.*

Customer's Page.

This page is for customers who enjoyed Adobe Audition CC Keyboard Shortcuts.

Our beloved and respectable reader, we thank you very much for your patronage. Please we will appreciate it more if you rate and review this book; that is if it was helpful to you. Thank you.

Download Our EBooks Today For Free.

In order to appreciate our customers, we have made some of our titles available at 0.00. They are totally free. Feel free to get a copy of the free titles.

Here are books we give to our customers free of charge:

(A) For Keyboard Shortcuts in Windows check:

Windows 7 Keyboard Shortcuts.

(B) For Keyboard Shortcuts in Office 2016 for Windows check:

Word 2016 Keyboard Shortcuts For Windows.

(C) For Keyboard Shortcuts in Office 2016 for Mac check:

<u>OneNote 2016</u> Keyboard Shortcuts For Macintosh.

Follow <u>this link</u> to download any of the titles listed above for free.

Note: Feel free to download them from our website or your favorite bookstore today. Thank you.

Other Books By This Publisher.

Titles for single programs under Shortcut Matters Series are not part of this list.

S/N	Title	Series
Series A: Limits Breaking Quotes.		
1	Discover Your Key Christian Quotes	Limits Breaking Quotes
Series B: Shortcut Matters.		
1	Windows 7 Shortcuts	Shortcut Matters
2	Windows 7 Shortcuts & Tips	Shortcut Matters
3	Windows 8.1 Shortcuts	Shortcut Matters
4	Windows 10 Shortcut Keys	Shortcut Matters
5	Microsoft Office 2007 Keyboard Shortcuts For Windows.	Shortcut Matters
6	Microsoft Office 2010 Shortcuts For Windows.	Shortcut Matters
7	Microsoft Office 2013 Shortcuts For Windows.	Shortcut Matters
8	Microsoft Office 2016 Shortcuts For Windows.	Shortcut Matters
9	Microsoft Office 2016 Keyboard Shortcuts For Macintosh.	Shortcut Matters
10	Top 11 Adobe Programs Keyboard Shortcuts	Shortcut Matters
11	Top 10 Email Service Providers Keyboard Shortcuts	Shortcut Matters
12	Hot Corel Programs Keyboard Shortcuts	Shortcut Matters

13	Top 10 Browsers Keyboard Shortcuts	Shortcut Matters
14	Microsoft Browsers Keyboard Shortcuts.	Shortcut Matters
15	Popular Email Service Providers Keyboard Shortcuts	Shortcut Matters
16	Professional Video Editing with Keyboard Shortcuts.	Shortcut Matters
17	Popular Web Browsers Keyboard Shortcuts.	Shortcut Matters

Series C: Teach Yourself.

1	Teach Yourself Computer Fundamentals	Teach Yourself
2	Teach Yourself Computer Fundamentals Workbook	Teach Yourself

Series D: For Painless Publishing

1	Self-Publish it with CreateSpace.	For Painless Publishing
2	Where is my money? Now solved for Kindle and CreateSpace	For Painless Publishing
3	Describe it on Amazon	For Painless Publishing

www.ingramcontent.com/pod-product-compliance
Lightning Source LLC
Chambersburg PA
CBHW061030050326
40689CB00012B/2751